Madagascar

Mary N. Oluonye

Carolrhoda Books, Inc. / Minneapolis

Photo Acknowledgments

Photos, maps, and artworks are used courtesy of: John Erste, pp. 1, 2–3, 14, 16–17, 20–21, 22–23, 28–29, 32–33, 37, 38–39; Laura Westlund, pp. 4, 33; © Victor Englebert, pp. 4, 6, 7, 8, 9, 16, 17, 20, 22, 25 (top), 26, 27, 28 (both), 29, 31, 34, 35, 40 (both), 41, 42, 43, 44; © Eugene G. Schulz, pp. 10, 11 (both), 12 (both), 13, 14, 18, 24, 25 (bottom), 36 (both), 45; p. 19 (inset), © Alton Halverson; © The American Lutheran Church, used by permission of Augsburg Fortress, pp. 19, 23; © H. Bradt/C.O.P., p. 30. Cover photo © Victor Englebert

Carolrhoda Books, Inc.
A Division of Lerner Publishing Group
241 First Avenue North
Minneapolis, Minnesota 55401 U.S.A.

Website address: www.lernerbooks.com

Library of Congress Cataloging-in-Publication Data

Oluonye, Mary N.
   Madagascar/ by Mary N. Oluonye
      p. cm. — (A ticket to)
   Includes index.
   Summary: Describes the people, government, geography, religion, language, customs, lifestyle, and culture of Madagascar.
      ISBN 1-57505-145-1 (lib. bdg. : alk. paper)
      1. Madagascar—Juvenile literature. [1. Madagascar.] I. Title. II. Series.
DT469.M25048 2000
969.1—dc21   99-38138

Manufactured in the United States of America
1 2 3 4 5 6 – JR – 05 04 03 02 01 00

Contents

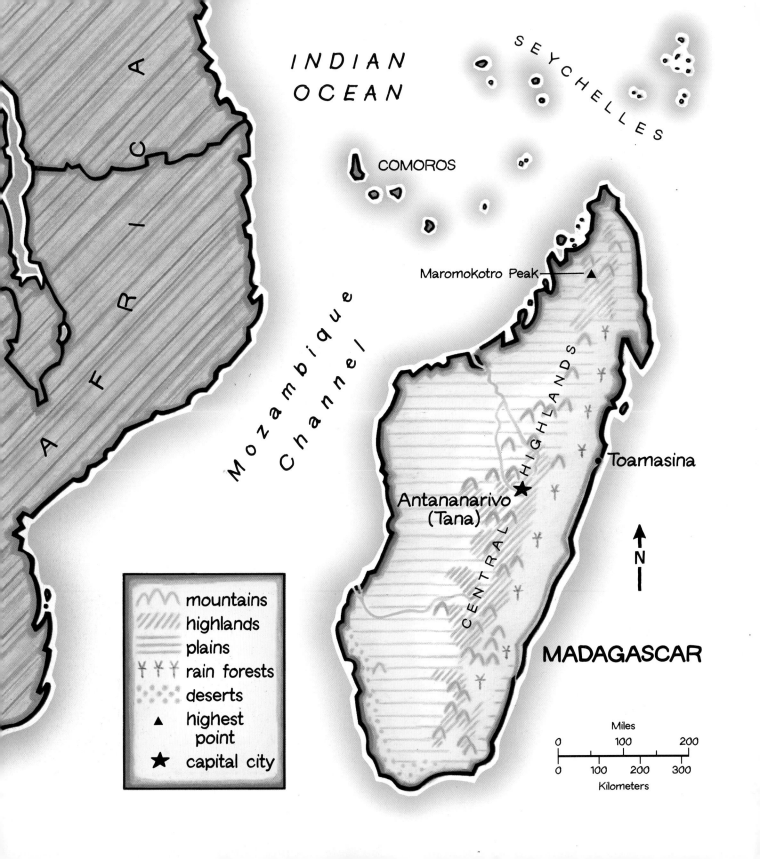

INDIAN
OCEAN

SEYCHELLES

COMOROS

Maromokotro Peak ——— ▲

Mozambique Channel

Toamasina

Antananarivo
(Tana) ★

CENTRAL HIGHLANDS

MADAGASCAR

N

⩗⩗⩗ mountains
////// highlands
===== plains
⅄⅄⅄ rain forests
∴∴∴ deserts
▲ highest
    point
★ capital city

Miles
0   100   200
0   100   200   300
Kilometers

Welcome!

Just off the coast of southeastern Africa, the country of Madagascar is easy to find. It is one of the biggest islands in the world.

The Mozambique **Channel** separates Madagascar and Africa. The Indian Ocean washes most of Madagascar's coast. The Mascarene Islands are to the east. Comoros is northwest, and Seychelles lies to the northeast.

MASCARENE
ISLANDS

Care for a swim? Watch out for sharks. They like to swim along Madagascar's coast, too.

The Evatra River begins in Madagascar's mountains and empties into the Indian Ocean.

The Land

Madagascar's western coast is a **plain** dotted with beaches and swamps. **Tropical rain forests** blanket the eastern coast, where the land flattens into coastal plains.

Mountains, hills, and valleys make up the Central Highlands. This region runs from north to south through the middle of Madagascar. The highest spot on the island, Maromokotro Peak, rises 9,436 feet.

Map Whiz Quiz

Take a look at the map on page 4. Trace the outline of Madagascar onto a piece of paper. Use a red crayon to color Madagascar. Can you find the Mozambique Channel? Color it blue and mark it with a "W" for west. How about Seychelles? Mark those islands with an "N" for north.

Broad plains stretch for miles across Madagascar. From this photo, it is easy to see why people call Madagascar the Great Red Island.

About the Weather

Dress to feel cool while you are in Madagascar. Even during July, the coolest month, temperatures hover around 65 degrees. The hot, rainy season—

Prepare to get wet during Madagascar's rainy summer!

The sun keeps Madagascar hot and dry from May to October, Madagascar's winter season.

Madagascar's summer—lasts from November to April. Then temperatures stay between 61 and 84 degrees. In the summertime, winds called **monsoons** blow from the Indian Ocean. Monsoons bring big storms that dump rain on Madagascar's eastern coast.

Amazing Animals

On the lookout for strange animals? Do not miss the lemurs! Of course, you will have to search for them after dark

Eek! A mouse lemur, one of the island's smaller lemurs, hangs out in a tree.

because that is when lemurs like to move around. They look like a mix between a monkey and a raccoon.

Madagascar is also home to huge fish called coelacanths. Coelacanths lived during the days of the dinosaurs!

Curious Creatures

Madagascar used to be a part of Africa. Long ago, it broke away. The living things on the island were cut off from the rest of the world. Plants and animals that died out in Africa continued to live, grow, and change in Madagascar.

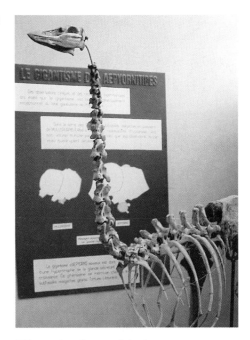

The elephant bird was a 10-foot-tall animal from Madagascar. It died out about 300 years ago.

How would you like to be green? Chameleons can change color to match their surroundings.

11

The periwinkle plant (above) cures many sicknesses. And the traveler's tree (left) can give you a drink! The trunk holds water that tastes yucky—but it will do if you are really thirsty.

Plants That Cure

Feel a cough coming on? Medicines made from plants found in Madagascar may be just what you need. For example, the periwinkle plant is in medicines that help people stop coughing. But that is not all! Periwinkle can also be used to treat diabetes, bleeding problems, sore throats, eye infections, and high blood pressure. Add katrafay, another local plant, to a hot bath to ease tired muscles.

These prickly plants grow in deserts on the southwestern part of the island. The plants' spiky thorns help keep away enemies.

*The people of Madagascar are called the Malagasy. Here some of them paddle a canoe like the ones their **ancestors** used to come to the island. How did your ancestors get to where you live?*

First People

The first people to live in Madagascar came from Southeast Asia as many as 1,500 years ago. They canoed 4,000 miles across the Indian Ocean and became the Malagasy people. Before long the Malagasy formed different **ethnic groups.** These groups had **traditions** that reflected where they lived on the island.

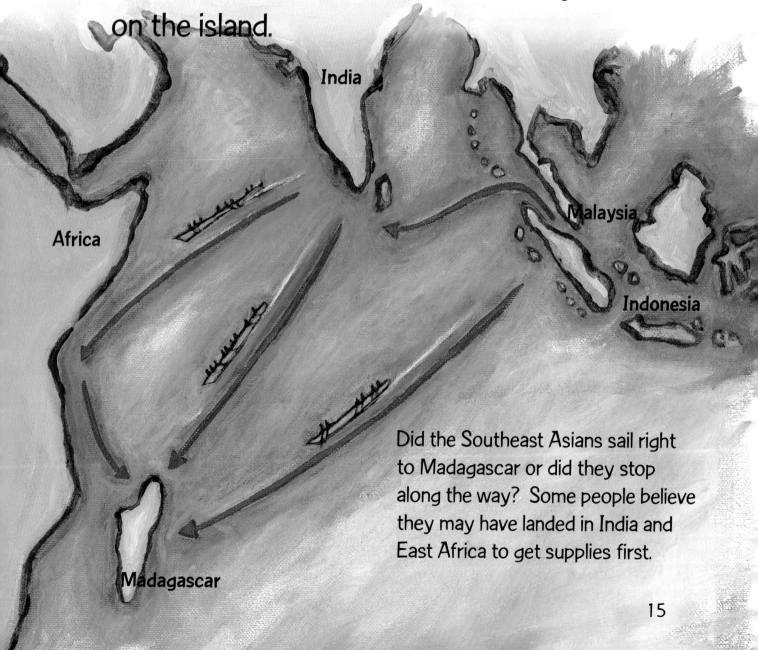

India

Africa

Malaysia

Indonesia

Madagascar

Did the Southeast Asians sail right to Madagascar or did they stop along the way? Some people believe they may have landed in India and East Africa to get supplies first.

15

This monument honors all of Madagascar's ethnic groups.

We Are Malagasy

Madagascar is home to 18 different ethnic groups! The Merina are the largest ethnic group in Madagascar. Many Merina work as storekeepers, businesspeople, lawyers, and doctors in the cities of the Central Highlands.

The Betsimisaraka
are fishers from the
coasts. They are
the second largest
group. The Betsileo
grow crops in the
Central Highlands.

A Betsileo sister and brother

Religion

On Sundays Malagasy Catholics go to this church to worship.

Almost half of all Malagasy are Christians. The other half follow the traditional religion of Madagascar. They believe that one god, Zanahary (Creator), rules everything. Lesser spirits live in animals, graves, houses, trees, and water. Ancestor worship is important in the traditional religion. Ancestors, known as *razana*, watch over living people and teach them right from wrong.

A tiny group of Malagasy are Muslims—followers of Islam. On Fridays they go to a mosque to pray.

The cattle horns that decorate this tomb are a sign of wealth. People who practice Madagascar's traditional religion might be buried in a grave like this one.

Speak to Me

The Malagasy people speak a language that is also called Malagasy. It shares words with Indonesian and African languages, as well as with Arabic, English, and French. The Malagasy alphabet looks like the English alphabet, but it

Madagascar's newspapers might be in French or Malagasy. Do the grown-ups in your house like to read the news? In what language are their papers written?

_q, u, w, x_ does not have the letters *c, q, u, w,* or *x.* Some people speak French. It was introduced when France ruled Madagascar for a short time. Malagasy and French are the island's two official languages.

Talk to a Malagasy

Here are a few words and phrases in Malagasy.

English	Malagasy	Pronunciation
Hello	Manoa ahoana	MAH-noh OHN
How are you?	Fahasalamana?	fah-sah-lah-MAHN-ah
Good-bye	Veloma	veh-LOOM
Yes	Eny	AY-nee
No	Tsia	TSEE-yah

Three men wear their lambas—a sign that they are probably Malagasy.

Lamba Time

What do you like to wear? Many Malagasy wear shorts and T-shirts. But some choose *lambas*, long scarves that they wrap around their bodies.

Malagasy women use a machine called a loom to weave lambas from silk, cotton, wool, or even grass. Weavers make lambas in all sorts of colors and sizes. Some lambas are patterned with pictures of landscapes, fruit, flowers, or geometric shapes.

A woman weaves a new lamba. Would you like to wear it when she is finished?

In the Country

All in the Family

Here are the Malagasy words for family members.

grandfather	*dadabe*	(dah-dah-BAY)
grandmother	*nenibe*	(neh-nee-BAY)
father	*dada*	(DAH-dah)
mother	*neny*	(NEE-nee)
uncle	*dadatoa*	(dah-dah-TOO-ah)
aunt	*nenitoa*	(nee-nee-TOO-ah)
son	*zanaka lahy*	(ZAH-nah-kah LYE)
daughter	*zanaka vavy*	(ZAH-nah-kah VAH-vee)
brother	*rahalahy*	(rah-hah-LAH-hee)
sister	*rahavavy*	(rah-hah-VAH-vee)

In Malagasy villages, kids live with parents, grandparents, great-grandparents, uncles, aunts, and cousins. Other family members usually live close by. Most country families grow their food in gardens.

A village woman carries her sleepy son in her lamba.

People and cows relax at the end of a long day.

City Life

Is your street as steep as this one in Antananarivo?

Busy Antananarivo is Madagascar's biggest city and the country's capital. Narrow, stone-paved streets and stairs wind between the houses and over hills. Railways and roads crisscross Toamasina, Madagascar's largest port city.

Lake Anosy sits right in the middle of Antananarivo. People like to call the city Tana as a nickname.

Many people living in Malagasy cities are poor. Grown-ups work hard to make enough money to buy food. Others do not have jobs and must spend the days begging for money.

On the Go

You can walk to the next town (above) or go on a taxi-brousse (left).

In a hurry? Then avoid cars in Madagascar. Poor roads make for a slow and bumpy ride. Lots of people just walk. Others may ride in a cart or wagon pulled by cows. In some cities, you can catch a ride in a *pousse pousse.*

A pousse pousse (which means "push push" in French) is a cart that a person pulls.

Pousse-pousse drivers have to pull hard! That is why you will not find these carts in hilly cities such as Tana.

Ceremony

Because ancestors are so important in Madagascar's traditional religion, people continue to take care of their

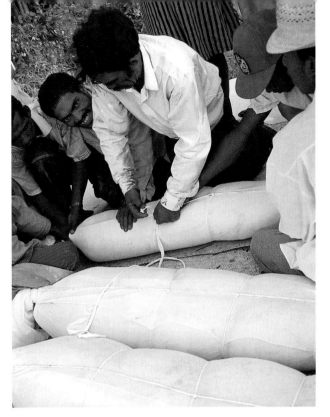

Famadihana can be sad, but it is also a time to eat, sing, and dance. These men bundle their ancestors in new lambas.

family members even after they have died. During a ceremony called *famadihana*, family members open the dead person's grave and remove the lamba he or she was wearing when buried. Then they wash the body and wrap it in a new silk lamba.

Sidetrack

Famadihana costs a lot of money. Families must pay for food and entertainment for the guests. That is why families only host the event when they can afford it—usually every three, five, or seven years.

After the ceremony, a family may return their ancestors to fancy tombs such as these.

Party Time

The Malagasy new year, called Alahamady, is a fun holiday. On New Year's Eve, people in Antananarivo dress up in lambas and walk to the highest point in the town. There they give each other gifts, listen to music, and sing. They may even try to talk to their ancestors. The next morning, many Christian Malagasy go to church.

Dear Mom and Dad,

Madagascar is a blast! Yesterday we climbed the royal hill of Ambohimanga in Tana to celebrate Alahamady—the Malagasy new year. Grandma even gave me a lamba to wear over my clothes. We listened to loud music and danced in the old queen's palace. It was so fun!

See you soon!

Freedom Fest

France used to rule Madagascar. In 1960 Madagascar became an independent country. The Malagasy celebrate their freedom each June 26. Schoolchildren sing the national anthem and parade through the streets with banners. In the evening, friends and family get together to dance and feast.

33

School

Alarm clocks ring early for Malagasy kids who have to make it to class by 7:00 A.M. All Malagasy children between the ages of 6 and 14 go to school. Instructors teach all classes in French. Pupils study English, science, math, history, and geography.

Malagasy kids take a test while their teacher paces the room.

At 10:00 A.M., kids go home for lunch and a rest. But they are not yet done for the day! At 3:00 they go back to class until 5:00.

Fady

In Madagascar, a set of rules called *fady* explain what people should not do. Here are a few examples of fady.

- Being rude to a stranger is fady.

- Refusing a stranger's kindness and hospitality is fady.

- Children eating their meals before their elders is fady.

Are you hungry? Try this Malagasy meal of rice, stew, and salad (above). For dessert, take a piece of sweet fruit (inset).

Rice Is Nice

Rice is the most popular food in Madagascar. Diners eat watery rice for breakfast. For lunch and dinner, folks feast on firmly cooked rice, served with vegetables or chicken, fish,

Tomatoes and green onions go into Madagascar's favorite salad, lasary voatabia.

or pork stews. Chili peppers, salt, curry powder, cloves, and garlic spice up the stews. A side dish called *lasary voatabia* is tasty. Cooks make it by tossing tomatoes and onions into a lemon and hot pepper sauce.

Tall Tales

Malagasy kids love to listen to **folktales.**
Many favorite stories try to explain how
the world came to be. Proverbs, called
ohabolana, are popular in Madagascar.
Malagasy speakers use lots of these short,
smart sayings when chatting with friends.
An example of ohabolana is, "Do not kick
away the canoe that helped you cross the
river." That means, "Do not forget the people
who helped you become successful in life."

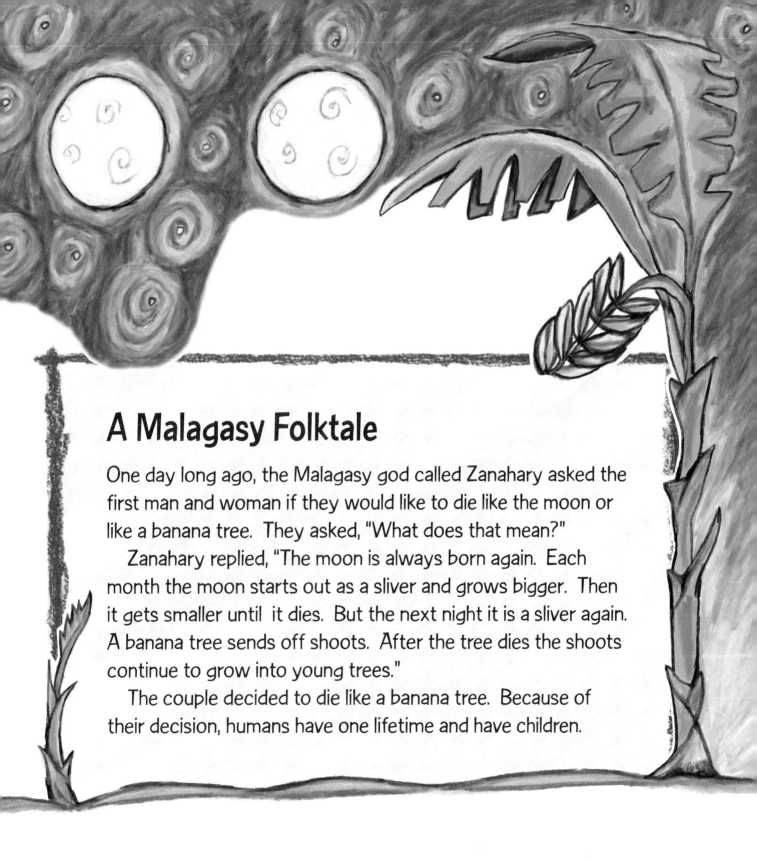

A Malagasy Folktale

One day long ago, the Malagasy god called Zanahary asked the first man and woman if they would like to die like the moon or like a banana tree. They asked, "What does that mean?"

Zanahary replied, "The moon is always born again. Each month the moon starts out as a sliver and grows bigger. Then it gets smaller until it dies. But the next night it is a sliver again. A banana tree sends off shoots. After the tree dies the shoots continue to grow into young trees."

The couple decided to die like a banana tree. Because of their decision, humans have one lifetime and have children.

Zoma Market

A woman weaves a basket out of palm leaves. Maybe you can use the basket to bring things home from Zoma Market!

An artist puts the finishing touches on his wood carving.

40

*Zoma means "Friday."
A long time ago, the
market was only open
on Fridays. But these
days, people can shop
there anytime.*

A great place to see lots of Malagasy
artwork is at Zoma Market in Antananarivo.
Zoma Market is the largest open-air market
in the world! Sellers display woven rugs,
mats, and hats. Also for sale are clothes,
wood carvings, musical instruments, toys,
furniture, food, and even magic charms.

Music in the Air

Malagasy music mixes styles from other regions. Many western Malagasy musicians like the strong drumbeats of African music. In the Central Highlands, people twang string instruments, making music like that of Southeast Asia.

On Sundays traveling musicians go from one Malagasy village to the next performing *hira gasy*. Hira gasy is a show that mixes storytelling, singing, and dancing. A speaker welcomes the audience with a speech called a *kabary*. Then actors sing and act out a play that teaches the audience a lesson about life. Dancers end the show by moving to the music of blaring horns, pounding drums, and singing violins.

Do you like to sing and dance? These Malagasy girls and boys sure do.

New Words to Learn

ancestor: A person from whom others are descended.

channel: A narrow strip of sea or ocean between two pieces of land.

ethnic group: A group of people with many things in common, such as language, religion, and customs.

folktale: A timeless story told by word of mouth from grandparent to parent to child. Many folktales have been written down in books.

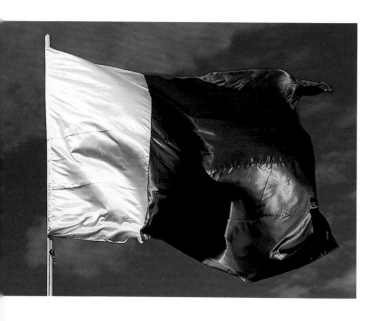

Each color in Madagascar's flag stands for something. White is for ideas. Red is for the country's independence. Green is for the people.

Rain forests once covered most of Madagascar. But people have cut down lots of the trees to make room for crops and farm animals.

monsoon: Strong, seasonal winds that sometimes carry heavy rainstorms.

plain: A large area of flat land.

tropical rain forest: A thick, green forest that gets lots of rain every year.

tradition: A way of doing things—such as preparing a meal, celebrating a holiday, or making a living—that a group of people share.

New Words to Say

Alahamady	ah-lah-MARD
Antananarivo	ahn-tah-nah-nah-REEV
Betsileo	BET-sihl-yoo
Betsimisaraka	BET-sih-MIH-shah-rahk
coelacanth	SEE-luh-kanth
fady	FAH-dee
famadihana	fah-mah-DEE-ahn
hira gasy	HEE-rah GASH
kabary	kah-BAHR
katrafay	kaht-rah-FYE
lasary voatabia	lah-sah-REE voh-tah-BEE
lemur	LEE-mehr
Mahafaly	mah-hah-FAH-lee
Malagasy	mahl-GASH
Maromokotro	mah-room-KOOT-roh
Merina	MAIR-n
ohabolana	uh-hah-boo-LAH-nah
pousse pousse	POOS POOS
razana	RAH-zah-nah
taxi-brousse	TAHK-see—BROOS
Toamasina	toh-MAH-see-nah
Zanahary	zah-nah-HAR
Zoma	ZOO-mah

More Books to Read

Darling, Kathy. *Chameleons: On Location.* New York: Lothrop, Lee, and Shepard Books, 1997.

Darling, Kathy. *Lemurs: On Location.* New York: Lothrop, Lee, and Shepard, 1998.

Dooley, Norah. *Everybody Cooks Rice.* Minneapolis: Carolrhoda Books, Inc., 1991.

Gutnik, Martin J. *Madagascar.* Madison, NJ: Raintree Steck-Vaughn, 1995.

Heale, Jay. *Madagascar.* New York: Marshall Cavendish, 1998.

Lasky, Kathryn. *Shadows in the Dawn: The Lemurs of Madagascar.* San Diego: Gulliver Books, 1998.

Rappaport, Doreen. *The New King.* New York: Dial Books for Young Readers, 1995.

Temko, Florence. *Traditional Crafts from Africa.* Minneapolis: Lerner Publications Company, 1996.

New Words to Find